CHERRY DENMAN

THE HISTORY PUZZLE

SINCLAIR~STEVENSON

First published in Great Britain in 1994
by Sinclair-Stevenson
an imprint of Reed Consumer Books Ltd
Michelin House, 81 Fulham Road, London SW3 6RB
and Auckland, Melbourne, Singapore and Toronto

A CIP catalogue record for this book is available
at the British Library
ISBN 1 85619 139 7

Typeset by Falcon Graphic Art Ltd
Printed and bound in China
Produced by Mandarin Offset

THE HISTORY PUZZLE

for
Barnaby

THE HISTORY PUZZLE

4,600
million years ago

600
million years ago

500
million years ago

400
million years ago

300
million years ago

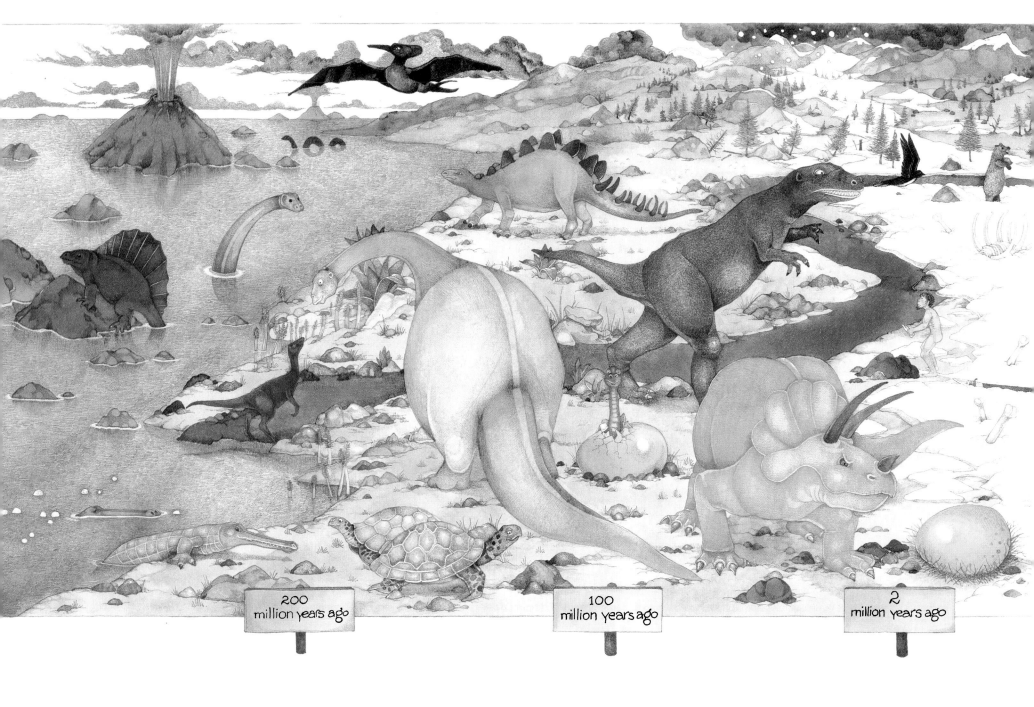

200
million years ago

100
million years ago

2
million years ago

10,000 years ago

3,000

1000

500

200

50

200

300

400

900

950

1000

1050

1150

1175

1200

1215

1225

1250

1310

1330

1350

1370

1390

1400

1410

1420

1480

1490

1500

1510

1660

1670

1740

1750

1790   1800   1810

1870 1880 1890 1900